This Earth Has Been Too Generous

poems by

Susan Marsh

Finishing Line Press
Georgetown, Kentucky

This Earth Has Been Too Generous

Copyright © 2022 by Susan Marsh
ISBN 978-1-64662-997-8 First Edition
All rights reserved under International and Pan-American Copyright Conventions. No part of this book may be reproduced in any manner whatsoever without written permission from the publisher, except in the case of brief quotations embodied in critical articles and reviews.

ACKNOWLEDGMENTS

The author wishes to thank the editors of publications in which the following poems have appeared, some in slightly different form:

Avocet, Thou Shall Not Reap
Clerestory, Equinox Storm; The River's Edge
Dark Matter: Women Witnessing, The Hunters; Elegy for the Cranes
Living Waters, Deepwater Horizon Disaster
Manzanita Quarterly, Grave Tending
Silver Birch Press, Waiting for the Rock to Sing
Wyoming Untrapped, The Hunters; Coyote

"Nonnezoshe" is a cento, borrowing from Zane Gray's account of going to Rainbow Bridge. The full account is widely available on the internet.

Publisher: Leah Huete de Maines
Editor: Christen Kincaid
Cover Art: Susan Marsh
Author Photo: Mary Lohuis
Cover Design: Elizabeth Maines McCleavy

Order online: www.finishinglinepress.com
also available on amazon.com

Author inquiries and mail orders:
Finishing Line Press
PO Box 1626
Georgetown, Kentucky 40324
USA

Table of Contents

Dawn Mugwort 1

The Spring Edition of Regret 2

Waiting for the Rock to Sing 3

Elegy for the Cranes 4

At the River's Edge 5

Early-onset Seriousness 6

Coyote 7

The Hunters 8

Thou Shall Not Reap 9

Nonnezoshe 10

Hooded Merganser 11

Asset Protection 12

Deepwater Horizon Disaster 13

Equinox Storm 14

On the Wings of Geese 15

Grave Tending 16

The Heart of the Matter 18

One Patch of Quilt 19

Lichen Ode 20

Islands 21

The Anthropocene 23

*In memory of my husband Don Plumley,
with whom I shared my love for the wild*

Dawn Mugwort

Buds in ranks of popcorn-white
Loose lenticulated branches: chokecherry.
Newborn lime green, raw sienna
Crimson-stained morning sky
The blue-green power of the wind.

Now dances free the flowered branch
As spruces endure like January days—
They have seen extravagance before.
They hide tanagers bright as summer
In the folds of their dusk-gray habits.

Respite from news of dissolution
Barefoot in damp morning grass
Toes hug the earth, grateful for its fortitude.
Before they're fully formed, a thousand
Supplications race to meet the sunrise.

Language leaves, thought dissolves.
Wordless prayers ascend to find their sisters—
Prayers for the wild and indigenous,
For the dreams of a man who hoped to be a judge
Broken by the judgment of a knee.

Medieval ramblers brought a piquant plant
To defend against evil and losing their way.
Bloom of the huntress, herb of the adventurer
Added to a mug of mead, it settled stormy souls.
A pilgrim for solace, I seek the path

Past words and thoughts and sorrows
In search of dawn mugwort.

The Spring Edition of Regret

Mountain exhales mist
Valley fills with its breath.
Beside a tarn I tarry
Above the clotted cold,
My flicker of faith unstable.

We live and grow and fall
Like autumn leaves.
For those who must always be right
For those who must choose sides
For those nobody knew,

The same tree keeps us standing
Its branches fragile as a sigh.

Waiting for the Rock to Sing

I am waiting for the rock to stir
poised here since a glacier
unceremoniously dumped it
on this lakeshore.
I am waiting to hear its tale
of an eons-long sojourn
from pluton to beach sand.

I am drawn to places that draw
no others. This weathered block
of granite lies far from a trail,
not the best view of the mountains.
I am drawn to the whistle of wings
cutting through a pre-dawn sky,
the tawny light of lake water
leaping among shadows,
the chorus of an untamed wind
among the polished peaks.

The miraculous does not hide
its splendor, yet it waits for no one.
This rock has sung its song forever
but I did not know the words.
Fog peels away like a rind
from the mountain front
revealing the surface of the lake
enchanting in its singular reflection.

Elegy for the Cranes

Reed grass sloughs, coverts of cottonwood and ash
Buffaloberry embroiders a ditch with threads of crimson fruit.
October spreads its wings, yearning for the sky's embrace.
Land flattens under cumulus and mare's tails
Blood-red lines of sunrise broaden to a saffron streak.

By noon the wind has turned, strong and from the north.
Primeval music tumbles from the vacant blue
And all at once the sky holds columns of pure grace,
Dozens of cranes bleating as they climb
The invisible staircase of the North Dakota sky.
One, at the far tip of a long chevron of birds,
Is white. Its wings ply the air like canvas sails,
Their hems dipped in the blackest ink.

Sunset lingers, sky empty without cranes.
This prairie was made for their millions,
Its silence for their cries. Twilight's fading violet
Shrouds ancient pathways aligned under the stars.
Tomorrow's sun will bleed again into the dawn,
The midday sky will wait the only way it knows—
Arms open, ardent, filled with light.

At the River's Edge

First daylight skims high snowfields
Dawn stirs blue among the pines.
Bugling elk, chortling ravens
The slow somber call of an owl.

Silence at the river's edge
Before the geese and cranes arise
Hidden in tall sedges, they hold fast
As suspended beads of rain.

Elk find refuge in the forest
I shelter behind a driftwood log
Rain-polished stones at the water's lip
O sweet small cup of sand.

Early-onset Seriousness

Envision me at two
     sitting in the Yakima River
          holding a dark round stone
Dad wants to take my picture
     asks me to look up
          I pull my head back
Short blond hair
     windblown halo of sunlight
          to offer him my best scowl.

A child with early-onset
     seriousness, who rarely smiled
          for cameras or for people,
Had no idea who she was
     who others were
          how could she fail to wonder?
The river cold against bare skin
     its water flowing clear and bright
          the smooth black volcanic cobble

Mystery enough
     steadfast enough
          complete enough.

She who sought the cold wild water
     hair flaring in a gust
          one shoulder warmed by sun
The other casting shadows
     over helgramites and cutthroats
          Felt the stirrings of a power
So essential it erased
     all traces of the trivial.
          It held her the way

She held a single river rock:
     mysterious, steadfast,
          complete.

Coyote

Coyote haunts the bottomlands,
Willow-weed and streamside braid
Vanishes and reappears
Not twenty feet away.

Intense amber eyes: my startled gaze
Slides away, by which I hope to say
I am neither predator nor prey.

The ages have cloaked coyote
In costumes that we choose,
Wise one, trickster, raven's twin.
Coyote grants us only two:

Devious or deadly. For we have shown
Ourselves as wicked, callous foes
Werewolves dressed in ovine clothes.

Before I take another breath
The coyote slips from sight
Stealth and silence are his ways
He doesn't pause to glance behind.

The Hunters

Where will the red-tails hunt,
razor-eyed on summer winds
when all this broken country
grows cul-de-sacs, not grain?
Where will the falcons stoop,
shadow splash on rough rock breaks
when the gear shafts of dead tractors
lie rusting in the rain?

The ribcage of a coyote hangs
on a three-strand barbwire gate
the wind has long since stolen
what the coyote came to raid.
Out here in these clay-hard hills,
here real estate is king
scavenging from dying farms
what sweat could not persuade.

The hunters are the first to hear:
Coyote, Hawk, goodbye.
Your shadows pass, swift and gone,
like a songbird in the falcon's eye.

Thou Shall Not Reap

> *A response to the painting Thou Shall not Reap the Corners of thy Field by Ron Kingswood, housed at the National Museum of Wildlife Art in Jackson, Wyoming.*

Thou shall not reap the corners of thy field
But yield an offering to those who came before
Those on wings and feathered feet,
With legs of four or six or eight
Who hunted the great prairie, stalked the cattail sloughs,
Who sought refuge in the underbrush
For countless millions knew this land
Before thy patriarch took possession
And subjected it to his mastery.

Thou shall not burn the limits of thy pasture
Ditches thick with native brush,
Abide instead this rough and unkempt row
For all who dwelt before thee, they who endured
For centuries before the rake and plow
And knew no fence or boundary.
Their seed was scattered on four winds
And filled the plains with grasses taller than a man
And made rich and fertile the soil that feeds thee.

Thou shall not reap the corners of thy field
But render unto ash and poplar this patch of wilding prairie
Tall bluestem swishing in the wind, hiding speckled eggs
And rare white orchid blossoms.
Thou shall stride out into the dawn,
Frost brushing at thy boots
And lie beside a hedgerow under the pale stars
And feel the ground fast beneath the temple of thy soul
The earth that sustains thee, the temple of all things.

Nonnezoshe

We rode all day between bluffs and ridges
The sand blew the dust rose.
Toward sunset a storm gathered to the north
Promising cool and sultry air.

A long canyon. Straight rugged red walls.
Black storm-clouds, the rumble of thunder.
A dazzling flash of lightning. Colossal shafts
And buttes of rock—monuments
Black against that strange horizon.

Limping, lagging, plodding. Wetherill waiting.
The dark and silent Indian beside him,
Looking down the canyon
Past the vast jutting wall. A mile beyond
All was bright with sunset

And spanning the canyon was a magnificent
Natural bridge, sweeping majestically from red walls,

Its iris-hued arch against the sky.

Hooded Merganser

Secretive and solitary, epitome of elegance
His slender bill, a razor in a scabbard
His head a crescent moon that spreads
Into an open fan, like my outspread hand.

Lophodytes: phantom crested diver
Whose name springs from the Sea of Crete,
Whose face evokes Ming lacquerware,
Black and white and gold cabochon of eye.

Water bulges against his moon-white breast
Before he slips below the pond's dark skin
Leaving not a ripple. He flies underwater
Brandishing his sawtoothed sword.

A bird the color of snow and winter water
Leaves me to wonder if I only dreamt him.
Will he emerge among the stately pintails
The gabbling crowds of mallards?

My feet lose their grip on frosty stones
My eyes search the closed door of the pond.
My heart seeks the master of this house
The duende, surging upward. I wait. I wait.

Asset Protection

Let us protect our assets:
Bright, laundry-day air
Water we can drink
A place to walk and daydream
The rush of water, the earth's eternal quiet.
A land we share
With those whose lives depend on it,
Including our own,
Including otters, eagles, bears.

Let us manage our wealth:
Land that can keep giving
To all who come to receive,
Fertile, stable soil
Creeks that meander and deepen
Sedges clutching their margins
Knitting them together,
Trout that daydream in their shadows
Forests that mature and decay
And spill their dividends to the future.
They will only grow in value.

Deepwater Horizon Disaster

A continent of oil
not an iceberg, not a slick,
the size of five states and growing
like a thunderhead it collapses
under its weight, raining
bronzed and iridescent tar
onto the ocean floor.
It rolls into the littoral zone with
bloated carcasses of dolphins.
Oystermen wring their kerchiefs
a fisherman mourns and sells
the skiff his father built by hand.
Volunteers wade into the sludge
trying to save a tern.

Who did this? We sharpen our fingers
for pointing. Big oil. Government
(asleep at the switch as usual), while
citizens look the other way
filling our tanks with two-dollar gas
and folding over the front page.
Addicted to oil, the president said,
and addicts we remain
watching from our fuel-warmed rooms
as the last of the priceless,
the irreplaceable, wash ashore. God weeps.

O Pelican, Sea Turtle, Man o'war.
There nothing we can do
to earn your forgiveness now.

Equinox Storm

Yesterday the aspens stood
In the raking light of afternoon
People stopped to watch as one
By one the glowing amber leaves
Broke free and floated down.

At dawn, the stern grasp
Of an autumn wind strips
The branches of their gold
Their damp remains lie
Cheerless as cold ashes.

Snow sifts from nowhere
Clings to trunks and pecks
Against the window.
The last blue folding chair
Sits askew under the trees

Its lap fills with
Solitude and leaves.

On the Wings of Geese

March arrives on the wings
Of twenty-five geese calling
As they float over the river.
Thin haze gathers into overcast,
The sun a bright thumbprint
Pressed into the cloud's gray gauze.

Chickadees compose their bell tones
To announce the end of the season
For handouts at bird feeders
And foraging for insects on the snow.
The first flocks of robins arrive,
Grizzlies emerge from winter dens.

The geese, already paired,
Beat their urgent paths upstream
To a particular patch of reeds
Beside a hidden pond
Soon to ring with the din of chorus frogs
That the goslings will hear from their eggs.

Grave Tending

Burying a crossbill in the garden
I paused to think of where to dig the hole
Where earlier souls didn't sleep already—
Our twenty-year-old cats and ten-year-old catfish,
The nestling warblers from last summer,
And others I did not mean to forget.

I found a place in the raspberry patch
Pale knobby shoots already seeking sky
The soil supple from years of fond attention
Now shrugging off the grip of months in ice.
My spade sank like a talon into the moist soil.

Each spring I grave-tend, planting snow peas
Over the cats and tropical fish and songbirds,
Raking leaves from the knuckles of the iris
And purple fists of columbine over the old dog,
Ground made holy by the ones who lie below.

One night, only a week dead,
His front paws stretched across my chest
I lay awake, not dreaming, in the bed
We moved downstairs his last few months
When he could barely hobble to his nest.

I clip the irises, rake the slick wet leaves
Feel once more the soft heft of his paws,
Recall his obstinate male-dog ways,
The hair between his pads gone white
Well before his fifteenth year,
And I hope the flowers will bloom well

More beautiful than ever for him, because of him
I hope the peas grow long and fat over the cats
The berries plump over the newly buried crossbill
And I wonder how I could ever know
Which among them I love best.

The Heart of the Matter

The river holds one deep pool
The one that wets your hem
As if it wants to pull you in. Resist.
If you go you may not return.

Procrastinate, lounge in the sun
Sketch water, trees and wildflowers.
The pool waits, dark and patient,
Keeping your secrets, truths and lies.

Flowers fade and go to seed, sun slides
Behind the mountain. Sit silent now,
On a boulder scoured by eternities
Of soft, pliant water.

It will soften your sharp edges too.
Don't be afraid; your heart lies there.
The sky saves its clearest blue
For the bottom of the pool.

One Patch of Quilt

We know about the way they treat the chickens
But on a budget, buy the cheaper eggs.
One man says wolves are meant for shooting,
Another lives with a wolf named Cucumber.
At the sight of a snake my mother grabbed the hoe.
I got there first, carried it to the woods and let it go.

Rescued from a backhoe's jaw, a rubber boa
Spent the winter eating crickets in a terrarium
Until it was warm enough to be set free.
The friend who kept it became an expert
In the ways of rubber boas, small shy snakes
Most of us have never seen.

It all comes down to empathy
One patch of quilt acknowledging the other
For we lie together with stiches tight,
The only escape an irreversible rending of the fabric.

Lichen Ode

O jewel lichen, with your galaxies of growth
Vermilion, cinnabar and jade
Denizen of the knife's edge, of stone
Not yet softened into soil, of cliffs
Exposed to winter's desiccating winds—
Your presence marks the borderline
Where the realm of the mineral yields
To the probing fingers of life.

Through a hand lens your random blotches
Form intricate lobes, water lapping at a shore
Cracks in desert mud flats, folds of fabric
Twirling like a dancer's skirt. Fireworks.
You set a course for wayward seeds
Whose roots find dark moist pockets
A home bequeathed by lichen.

O lichen, with your splash of splendor
You draw me when all is end-of-winter gray.
My notice is more than academic; it's
Visceral, bubbling from the deep human well
Of yearning for fellow living things.
I zoom in with loupe and camera lens
To capture your cups of asci raised
Like tiny chalices: This is my blood.

Resolute, you reach for what you cannot see,
Blazing trails across barrens of indifferent stone.
My camera's field of view fills
With your patient pinch of life
As I am filled with wonder at
Your interweaving, ever-changing
Polychromism, like a child peering
Down the tube of a kaleidoscope
For the first time.

Islands

I want to know there are islands
no one has ever seen.
Islands undiscovered, unexplored
innocent of disease and infection
and species that don't belong.

I want to know there are winds
enough to repel compounds
that don't belong in ocean air,
waves enough to sweep the beaches
clean of toxic flotsam.

Waves and winds and islands
headlands still above the sea
rising all around them, cliffy
and dotted with the nests of
albatross and tern, seabirds
whose bellies bulge with squid
whose babies don't eat plastic.

I want to say
that I would never go there,
don't want a map or photograph
I already have a picture
in my mind, as do you,
of unspoiled unsullied strands.
My islands lack sparkling beaches
with palms overhanging
clear pearl-strewn lagoons.

I am fine with imposing lumps
of sharp volcanic rock, that
with their sheer curmudgeonliness
keep us at bay, warn us away.
Thumbs up to windblown archipelagoes

scrub and cactus, sulfurous fumaroles
sea ice piled like broken platters
on frozen Arctic shores.

I want to say
this earth has been too generous
oceans too blue, beaches too white
continents too green, welcoming
each species, including one
that plows all others under
leaving only the most inaccessible
of sea stacks and atolls.

The uninhabitable:
the deepest depths the highest peaks.
I want to know
that islands of austerity
refuges for wildness
still abide, if only in my mind.

The Anthropocene

When did people transform into human resources?
When did our home planet become a treasury to plunder?
I missed those events: I am still me
The earth still holds my steps.

A few hundred million years hence, intelligent life
May find the remains of the Anthropocene. A layer
Thin as a varve, a sheet of foil
A small misstep corrected.

Susan Marsh lives in Jackson, Wyoming. She has combined her interests in writing and natural history in a body of work that explores the relationship of humans to the wild. Her poems have appeared in *Clerestory, Manzanita Review, Dark Matter, Silver Birch* and other journals. Her non-fiction work has appeared in publications that include *Orion, North American Review,* and *Fourth Genre,* and in many anthologies. Books include an award-winning novel, *War Creek,* and ten non-fiction books, including *A Hunger for High Country* and *Saving Wyoming's Hoback,* winner of the Wallace Stegner Prize in Environmental Humanities. She writes a column "Back to Nature" for *Mountain Journal.*

www.ingramcontent.com/pod-product-compliance
Lightning Source LLC
LaVergne TN
LVHW041520070426
835507LV00012B/1717